CROSS STITCH
ANIMALS

Also by Jana Hauschild Lindberg and published by Cassell:

Making Gifts in Counted Cross Stitch (1990)
Flowers in Cross Stitch (1992)

CROSS STITCH
ANIMALS
Most than 60 captivating designs
from the world of nature

JANA HAUSCHILD LINDBERG

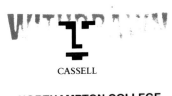

CASSELL

A CASSELL BOOK

First published 1994
by Cassell
Villiers House
41/47 Strand
London
WC2N 5JE

Distributed in the United States
by Sterling Publishing Co., Inc.
387 Park Avenue South, New York, NY 10016-8810

Distributed in Australia
by Capricorn Link (Australia) Pty Ltd
2/13 Carrington Road, Castle Hill, NSW 2154

British Library Cataloguing-in-Publication Data
A catalogue record for this book is available from the British Library

ISBN 0-304-34296-3

Typeset by MS Filmsetting Limited, Frome, Somerset

Printed and bound in Great Britain by Bath Colour Books

Contents

Introduction

Since the beginning of time, human beings have enjoyed depicting the animals surrounding them. Even cave-dwellers painted on the walls of the caves in which they lived, creating decorations which we can still appreciate today. For one chapter of this book I have taken the liberty of transforming some historic works of art into cross stitch so that we can enjoy them as adornments in our homes. Other chapters are filled with my own designs representing the whole spectrum of the animal kingdom — beasts, birds, insects and fish. Use them to decorate your home, following the accompanying project ideas, and you will be carrying on a tradition established by our ancestors thousands of years ago.

Counted Cross Stitch
Technique and Projects

Counted cross stitch is one of the simplest forms of embroidery. It consists of a series of crossed stitches embroidered on an evenweave fabric over the intersection of the horizontal and vertical threads. The stitches are worked following a chart. Each cross stitch is indicated by a symbol; the different symbols represent different colours (fig. 1). You can work the design as directed in the colour key, or make up your own original colour scheme.

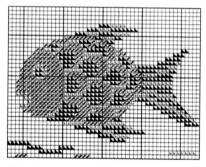

(Fig. 1)

FISH

- ◤ 797 dark blue
- ◪ 807 dark turquoise
- ⌊ 598 light turquoise

The size of a cross stitch design is determined by the type of fabric upon which it is embroidered. Although finished sizes are given for the designs in this book, it is easy to calculate what a different finished size will be by using the following formula:

$$\text{Finished size} = \frac{\text{Number of stitches}}{\text{Thread-count of fabric}}$$

For example, let's say you have selected a design that is 42 stitches wide and 98 stitches long and you would like to work on a cloth that has $5\frac{1}{2}$ threads per cm (14 threads per in). The finished width of your design can be determined by dividing the number of stitches (42) by the number of threads ($5\frac{1}{2}$/14), which gives you a design that is 7.5 cm (3 in) wide. For the length, divide the number of stitches (98) by the thread count ($5\frac{1}{2}$/14) to find out that the design will be 17.5 cm (7 in) long. If you feel this size is too large, try switching to a linen cloth which has 10 threads per cm (25 threads per in). The size in that case would be approximately 4 cm ($1\frac{1}{2}$ in) wide by 10 cm (4 in) long. Use this formula to decide quickly which thread count of fabric is best for you to use.

MATERIALS

FABRIC

You can use any evenweave fabric made from cotton, linen, wool or synthetic blends. Cotton and linen fabrics are the most widely used. Counted-thread fabrics specially woven for cross stitch, such as Aida or Hardanger, are available in many needlecraft shops, although these are limited in colour range. Aida fabric is cotton and can be bought in three sizes: $4\frac{1}{2}$, $5\frac{1}{2}$ or 7 stitches per cm (11, 14 or 18 stitches per in). Hardanger cloth is available in linen or cotton. If you would like to embroider on an unusual-coloured fabric, try using linen which is available in most fabric shops. When using linen, one has to take into account the inevitable slubs and inconsistencies that occur in the weave; this is why it is best to work counted cross stitch over two or more threads on linen fabric (see fig. 7). Thirty-count linen will give much the same effect as working on 14-count Aida cloth.

The materials used for the designs given in this book include linen and Aida. Linen measures are in threads. Aida measures are in stitches. Please note the following:

10 threads per cm = 25 per in
8 threads per cm = 20 per in
6 threads per cm = 15 per in

$5\frac{1}{2}$ stitches per cm = $13\frac{1}{2}$ per in
$4\frac{1}{2}$ stitches per cm = 11 per in

THREADS AND YARNS

Six-strand cotton embroidery floss is ideal for counted cross stitch because the floss can be separated into the exact number of strands that provide the correct amount of coverage. Use thread or yarn that is the same thickness as the threads of the fabric you are embroidering. For flatter designs, separate the strands of floss and work with two strands in your needle. If you wish to create a more textured effect, use more strands. You can also use silk or metallic threads, Danish Flower Thread, pearl cotton, even crewel wool, depending on the

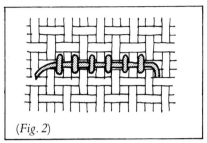

(Fig. 2)

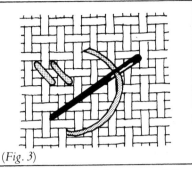

(Fig. 3)

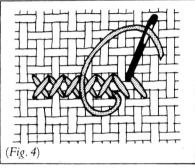

(Fig. 4)

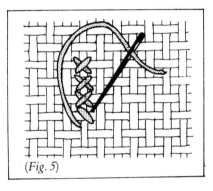

(Fig. 5)

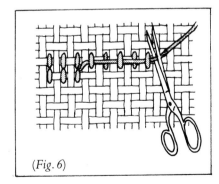

(Fig. 6)

thread count of your fabric. To add some sparkle to a design, mix one strand of metallic thread with two strands of embroidery floss. Throughout this book I have referred to DMC six-strand embroidery floss. A conversion chart at the end of this chapter shows at a glance where you can make substitutions with flosses manufactured by two other companies: Royal Mouliné, or Coats/Bates Anchor.

EQUIPMENT

NEEDLES
Use a small blunt tapestry needle, size number 24 or 26, to avoid splitting the fabric threads.

HOOP
Work with a small round embroidery hoop which consists of an inner ring and an adjustable outer ring that tightens by turning a screw.

SCISSORS
You must have a pair of small sharp embroidery scissors for cutting threads and a pair of sharp fabric shears for cutting out the fabric.

TECHNIQUE

Depending upon the gift project that you would like to make (see instructions at the end of this chapter), cut your fabric to the desired size plus about 2.5 cm (1 in) around each of the edges. Overcast the edges of the fabric to prevent unravelling by hemming, zigzagging on the sewing machine or

whipstitching. Find the centre of the fabric by folding it in half crosswise and lengthwise; mark the centre point with a small stitch. Then find the centre of your design (usually indicated on the charts by arrows). Do not begin your design at the centre; instead, count the number of squares on the chart from the centre point to the top, then count the same number of squares to the top of your fabric and work your first stitch there. Work the design in horizontal rows of colour from left to right. Place the fabric in the embroidery hoop so that it is taut. Adjust the tension as you work so that the fabric is always firmly held.

Begin stitching by leaving a length of waste thread on the back of the work, securing it with your first few stitches. Fig. 2 shows how the waste thread is secured on the wrong side of the work. Insert your needle into the holes of the fabric, working one slanted stitch over the intersection of two threads from lower right to upper left as shown in fig. 3. Continue working the required number of slanting stitches across the row, following the symbols on the chart. Then work back across the row, making slanting stitches from lower left to upper right to finish each cross stitch as shown in fig. 4. (In Denmark and America, stitches are worked from lower left to upper right, then crossed from lower right to upper left. It makes no difference which way you stitch, as long as all the stitches are crossed in the same direction.)

When you are working a vertical row of stitches, cross each stitch in turn as shown in fig. 5. To end a line of stitching, finish your last stitch and keep the needle and thread on the wrong side of the work. Wiggle the

point of the needle beneath a few threads on the wrong side and pull the thread through as shown in fig. 6; clip off the excess thread so that the ends will not show through on the right side of the work.

If you are working on linen, or if you wish to make larger stitches, work over two sets of threads in each direction as shown in fig. 7. Your first few stitches may be difficult, but once you have established a row of stitches, you'll have no trouble counting two threads instead of one.

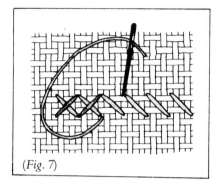

(Fig. 7)

BACKSTITCH

Backstitch is very commonly used in conjunction with counted cross stitch to outline, delineate features or emphasize a portion of the design. Work the backstitches from one hole to the next in a horizontal, vertical or diagonal direction; see fig. 8.

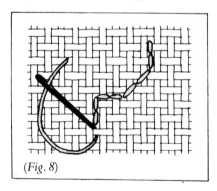

(Fig. 8)

WORKING WITH WASTE CANVAS

Counted cross stitch can be worked on non-evenweave fabrics by using a non-interlock waste canvas. Select a canvas with a stitch count of the desired size. Cut the canvas slightly larger than the finished size of your design. Baste the canvas to your chosen fabric in the area you wish to embroider. Using a crewel or chenille needle, work the design over the canvas. As you work, pass the needle straight up and down through the

fabric and canvas; take great care not to catch the canvas threads in your embroidery. When the embroidery is finished, remove the basting and dampen the canvas thoroughly using a warm wet towel. Gently pull out the canvas threads one by one. Iron the finished embroidery.

SMALL QUICK PROJECTS

BOOKMARK

Cut a piece of evenweave fabric about 15 × 5 cm (6 × 2 in). Overcast the raw edges. Embroider a small motif or border design on the fabric; gently iron the finished embroidery. Trim away the overcast edges. Carefully draw away threads from the cut edges, creating a 6 mm (¼ in) fringe.

GIFT TAG, PLACECARD OR NAME LABEL

Cut evenweave fabric 2.5 cm (1 in) larger than the desired finished size. Overcast the raw edges. Embroider a small motif on the fabric; gently iron the finished embroidery. Cut away excess fabric, leaving about 13 mm (½ in) all around the edge of the design. Carefully draw away threads from the cut edges, creating a 6 mm (¼ in) fringe. Glue the wrong side of the design to a piece of card.

PINCUSHION OR SACHET

Cut evenweave fabric about 2.5 cm (1 in) larger than the desired finished size (or more, depending upon the size of the design). Overcast the raw edges. Embroider a small motif on the fabric, gently iron the finished embroidery. Cut away excess fabric to the desired size. Cut a matching

piece of fabric for the back; stitch together with right sides facing and raw edges even, making a 6 mm (¼ in) seam and leaving an opening for turning. Turn to the right side and stuff with kapok, fibrefill or potpourri until plump. Fold in the raw edges at the opening and slipstitch the opening closed.

MATCHBOX COVER

Embroider a small motif on a piece of evenweave fabric; gently iron the finished embroidery. Cut away excess fabric to the exact size of the matchbox you wish to decorate. Glue the wrong side of the design to the top of the matchbox, making sure the raw edges are securely glued so that they do not unravel.

POCKET

Using a commercial pocket pattern, cut one pocket from evenweave fabric, adding the appropriate seam allowances. Embroider a small motif in the centre of the fabric; gently iron the finished embroidery. Cut a matching piece of fabric for the lining; stitch together with right sides facing, leaving an opening for turning. Turn to the right side, fold in the raw edges at the opening, and slipstitch the opening closed. Iron carefully. Topstitch the edges of the pocket if desired, then sew to the front of a blouse or skirt with small slipstitches.

TIE OR COLLAR

Read the earlier instructions for working with waste canvas. Select a small design. Centre the waste canvas on a tie or collar and baste into place. Work the design over the canvas, then remove the canvas threads as directed. Iron the finished embroidery gently.

HANDKERCHIEF

Read the earlier instructions for working with waste canvas. Select a small design. Position the waste canvas in the corner of a handkerchief and baste in place. Work the design over the canvas, then remove the canvas threads as directed. Iron the finished embroidery gently.

T-SHIRT

Read the earlier instructions for working with waste canvas. Select a medium to large design. Centre the waste canvas on the front of a T-shirt and baste in place. Work the design over the canvas, then remove the canvas threads as directed. Iron the finished embroidery gently.

BABY'S BIB

Use a piece of evenweave fabric, adding 6 mm ($\frac{1}{4}$ in) all round. Overcast the raw edges. Find the centre of the bib at the neckline; begin working a small design about 2.5 cm (1 in) below the raw neck edge or in the exact centre of the bib front. Gently iron the finished embroidery. Trim away the overcast edge. Finish the raw edges of the bib with bias binding, leaving excess binding at the back for tying.

CHRISTMAS ORNAMENTS

Cut evenweave fabric about 2.5 cm (1 in) larger than the desired finished size. Overcast the raw edges. Embroider a small motif on the fabric; gently iron the finished embroidery. Cut away excess fabric to the desired size; for a special effect, cut around the shape of the design, leaving a 6 mm ($\frac{1}{4}$ in) seam allowance all around. Cut a matching piece of fabric for the back; stitch together with right sides facing and raw edges

even, making a 6 mm ($\frac{1}{4}$ in) seam and leaving an opening for turning. Clip any curved edges. Turn to the right side and stuff with kapok or polyester fibrefill until plump. Fold in the raw edges at the opening and slipstitch the opening closed.

DECORATING THE HOME

WALLHANGING

Calculate the finished size of your design using the formula on page 8; cut evenweave fabric 5 cm (2 in) larger all round than the calculated size. Overcast the raw edges. Find the exact centre of the fabric and the design and count up to the top of the design and fabric. Begin embroidering downward until the design is finished. Carefully iron the finished embroidery. Measure 3.5 cm (1$\frac{1}{2}$ in) from the outer edge of the embroidery at the sides and bottom and trim away the excess fabric. Trim away only the overcast edge at the top. Fold the fabric at the side and bottom edges 6 mm ($\frac{1}{4}$ in) to the wrong side, then fold the fabric again 13 mm ($\frac{1}{2}$ in) to the wrong side. Baste, then sew the hem in place with small slipstitches. For the casing at the top edge, press the raw edge 6 mm ($\frac{1}{4}$ in) to the wrong side, then fold down 19 mm ($\frac{3}{4}$ in); stitch in place with small slipstitches. Iron gently. Insert a brass or wooden rod through the casing.

TABLE RUNNER

Cut a piece of evenweave fabric 2.5 cm (1 in) larger all around than the desired finished size of your table runner. Overcast the raw edges.

Decide where you wish to place the design. Embroider your chosen design, adding a border all around the table runner if desired. Carefully iron the finished embroidery. Cut away excess fabric, leaving 19 mm ($\frac{3}{4}$ in) for hemming. Fold the fabric 6 mm ($\frac{1}{4}$ in) to the wrong side, then fold the fabric again, this time 13 mm ($\frac{1}{2}$ in) to the wrong side. Baste, then sew the hem in place with small slipstitches. Iron gently.

CURTAIN TIEBACK OR LAMPSHADE TRIM

Cut evenweave fabric slightly longer than required and wide enough for the design plus 13 mm ($\frac{1}{2}$ in). Overcast the raw edges. Embroider a border design along the centre of the fabric. Gently iron the finished embroidery. Cut a matching piece of interfacing and lining. Baste the interfacing to the wrong side of the embroidery. With right sides facing, stitch the lining to the embroidery making a 13 mm ($\frac{1}{2}$ in) seam. Turn right side out and iron lightly. For the tieback, fold the raw edges inside and slipstitch in place. Apply Velcro touch-and-close fastener to secure the ends together. For the lampshade trim, fold the raw edges at one end to the wrong side. Slipstich or glue the embroidery around the bottom edge of the lampshade, slipping the raw edges inside the folded edge. Slipstitch to secure.

CURTAIN

Measure your window and make a curtain using an evenweave fabric; the curtain should not be very full. Hem the bottom edge of the curtain, but not the sides. Overcast the raw edges. Begin working a border design in the exact centre of the fabric, just above the hem. Work

outward to each side edge. When finished, hem the side edges of the curtain. Gently press the finished embroidery.

CUSHION

Calculate the finished size of your design using the formula on page 8; cut evenweave fabric 2.5 cm (1 in) larger than the calculated size all around. Overcast the raw edges. Work the design in the centre of the fabric. Carefully iron the finished embroidery. Trim away the excess fabric leaving a 13 mm ($\frac{1}{2}$ in) seam allowance all around. Cut a matching piece of fabric for the back. With right sides facing, stitch the back to the front, making a 6 mm ($\frac{1}{4}$ in) seam and leaving an opening for turning. Turn to the right side and stuff with kapok or polyester fibrefill until plump. Fold in the raw edges at the opening and slipstitch the opening closed; alternatively fit a zipper.

BATH TOWEL EDGING

Cut evenweave fabric slightly longer than your towel and wide enough for the design plus 13 mm ($\frac{1}{2}$ in). Overcast the raw edges. Embroider a border design along the centre of the fabric. Gently iron the finished embroidery. Trim off the overcast edges. Fold the raw edges of the embroidery 6 mm ($\frac{1}{4}$ in) to the wrong side and baste to your towel; slipstitch securely along each edge.

FOR THE KITCHEN AND DINING ROOM

POTHOLDER

Cut a piece of evenweave fabric about 18–23 cm (7–9 in) square. Overcast the raw edges. Select a design that will fit nicely on the fabric and embroider the design in the centre. Gently iron the finished embroidery. Trim off the overcast edges, then cut padding and a back to the same size; use two to three layers of cotton or wool padding (do not use polyester). Sandwich the padding between the embroidery and the back; baste the edges together. Use bias binding to finish the edges of the potholder, allowing excess binding at one corner to make a hanging loop.

SHELF BORDER

Cut evenweave fabric slightly longer than your shelf and wide enough for the design plus 13 mm ($\frac{1}{2}$ in). Overcast the raw edges. Embroider a border design along the centre of the fabric. Gently press the finished embroidery. Trim off the overcast edges. Cut a matching piece of interfacing. Baste the interfacing to the wrong side of the embroidery.

Fold the raw edges of the embroidery 6 mm ($\frac{1}{4}$ in) to the wrong side and secure to the interfacing with small slipstitches. Iron lightly. Pin or glue the border to the front of your cupboard shelf.

PLACEMAT

Cut a piece of evenweave fabric 2.5 cm (1 in) larger all round than the desired finished size of your placemat; a good finished size is about 35 × 45 cm (13$\frac{3}{4}$ × 17$\frac{3}{4}$ in). Overcast the raw edges. Decide where you wish to place the design—an attractive arrangement is to centre the design between the top and bottom edges along the left-hand edge of the fabric. Embroider your chosen design, adding a border all around the placemat if desired. Carefully iron the finished embroidery. Cut away excess fabric, leaving 19 mm ($\frac{3}{4}$ in) for hemming. Fold the fabric 6 mm ($\frac{1}{4}$ in) to the wrong side, then fold the fabric again, this time 13 mm ($\frac{1}{2}$ in) to the wrong side. Baste, then sew the hem in place with small slipstitches. Iron gently.

ROUND TABLECLOTH OR CENTREPIECE

Calculate the finished size of your design using the formula on page 8; cut evenweave fabric 3.5 cm (1½ in) larger than the calculated size all round. Overcast the raw edges. Find the exact centre of the fabric and the design; mark on the fabric with a basting thread. Count from the centre of the graph and the fabric to start the design. Work the graph, which is one-quarter of the design, as shown on page 110. Then turn the fabric clockwise and work the next quarter. Continue turning and repeating the quarter pattern twice more until the design is finished. Carefully iron the embroidery. Measure 3 cm (1¼ in) away from the outer edge of the embroidery and trim off the excess fabric. Fold the fabric 6 mm (¼ in) to the wrong side twice. Baste, then sew the hem in place with small slipstitches. Iron gently.

ROUND DOILY OR TRAYCLOTH

Work as for the tablecloth, but cut your evenweave fabric 2.5 cm (1 in) larger than the calculated size of the project all round.

Six-strand embroidery cotton (floss) conversion chart

Key: T = Possible substitute   ★ = Close match   − = No match

DMC	Royal Mouliné	Bates/Anchor	DMC	Royal Mouliné	Bates/Anchor	DMC	Royal Mouliné	Bates/Anchor	DMC	Royal Mouliné	Bates/Anchor	DMC	Royal Mouliné	Bates/Anchor	DMC	Royal Mouliné	Bates/Anchor
White	1001	2	437	8200★	362	680	6260★	901	816	2530	44★	936	5260T	269	3326	2115★	25★
Ecru	8600	926	444	6155★	291	699	5375	923★	817	2415T	19	937	5260	268	3328	2045	11★
208	3335★	110★	445	6000	288	700	5365★	229	818	2505★	48	938	8430	381	3340	—	329
209	3415★	105	451	—	399★	701	5365★	227	819	2000	892★	939	4405	127	3341	—	328
210	3320★	104	452	—	399★	702	5330	239	820	4345	134	943	4935★	188★	3345	5025T	268★
211	3410	108★	453	1015T	397★	703	5320	238	822	8605★	387★	945	8020★	347★	3346	5220T	257★
221	2570	897★	469	5255	267★	704	5310★	256★	823	4400★	150	946	7230★	332★	3347	5210★	266★
223	2555	894	470	5255★	267	712	8600★	387★	824	4225	164★	947	7255★	330★	3348	5270★	265
224	2545	893	471	5245	266★	718	3015★	88	825	4215	162★	948	8070	778★	3350	2220	42★
225	2540	892	472	5240	264★	720	—	326	826	4210	161★	950	8020T	4146	3354	2210	74★
300	8330	352★	498	2425T	20★	721	—	324★	827	4605	159★	951	8020T	366★	3362	—	862★
301	8315★	349★	500	5125	879★	722	—	323★	828	4850	158★	954	5455★	203★	3363	—	861★
304	2415★	47★	501	5120★	878	725	6215	306★	829	5825	906	955	5450	206★	3364	—	843★
307	6005★	289★	502	5110	876	726	6150★	295	830	5825★	889★	956	2170★	40★	3371	8435	382
309	2525★	42★	503	5105	875	727	6135	293	831	5825T	889★	957	2160T	40★	3607	—	87★
310	1002	403	504	5100	213★	729	6255	890	832	5815	907	958	—	187	3608	—	86
311	4275T	149★	517	—	169★	730	—	924★	833	5815★	874★	959	—	186	3609	—	85
312	—	147★	518	4860★	168★	731	—	281★	834	5810★	874	961	2515★	76★	3685	2335	70★
315	3130	896★	519	4855T	167★	732	5925T	281★	838	8425★	380	962	2515	76★	3687	2325	69★
316	3120	895★	520	—	862★	733	—	280★	839	8560	380★	963	2505	49★	3688	2320	66★
317	1030★	400★	522	—	859★	734	—	279★	840	8555	379★	964	—	185	3689	2310	49
318	1020★	399★	523	—	859★	738	8245★	942	841	8550	378★	966	5150★	214★	3705	—	35★
319	5025	246★	524	—	858★	739	8240★	885★	842	8505	376★	970	7040	316★	3706	—	28★
320	5015	216★	535	1115T	401★	740	7045	316★	844	1115★	401★	971	7045	316★	3708	—	26★
321	2415	47	543	8500	933★	741	6125	304	869	8720★	944★	972	6120★	298	48	9000★	1201★
322	—	978★	550	3380★	102★	742	6120	303	890	5025★	879★	973	6015	290	51	9014	1220
326	2530★	59★	552	3370★	101	743	6210	297	891	2135	35★	975	8365	355★	52	9006	1208
327	3365★	101★	553	3360	98	744	6110★	301★	892	2130	28	976	8355	308★	53	—	—
333	—	119	554	3355★	96★	745	6105	300★	893	2125★	27	977	8350	307★	57	9002	1203
334	4250T	145	561	—	212★	746	6100	386★	894	2115T	26	986	5430	246★	61	9013T	1218★
335	2525T	42★	562	—	210★	747	4850	158★	895	5430★	246★	987	5020T	244★	62	9000T	1201★
336	4270★	149★	563	—	208★	754	8075	778★	898	8425★	360	988	5295T	243★	67	—	1211★
340	—	118	564	—	203★	758	8080	868	899	2515	27★	989	5405T	242★	69	—	1218★
341	—	117	580	5935	267★	760	2035	9★	900	7230★	333	991	5165T	189★	75	9002	1206★
347	2425★	13★	581	5925	266★	761	2030	8★	902	—	72★	992	4925★	187★	90	9012★	1217
349	2400	13	597	4860★	168★	762	1010★	397★	904	5295★	258★	993	4915★	186★	91	9008★	1211
350	2045T	11	598	4855★	167★	772	—	264★	905	5295	258★	995	4710	410	92	9011T	1216★
351	2015T	11★	600	2225★	59★	775	4600★	128★	906	5285★	256★	996	4700	433	93	9007★	1210★
352	2015	10★	601	2225★	78★	776	2110★	24★	907	5280★	255	3011	5525T	845★	94	9011★	1216
353	2020★	8★	602	2640★	77★	778	3110	968★	909	5370	229	3012	5525★	844★	95	9006T	1208★
355	8095	5968	603	2720★	76★	780	8215★	310★	910	5370★	228★	3013	5515	842★	99	9005T	1207★
356	8090	5975★	604	2710	75★	781	8215	309★	911	5465★	205★	3021	—	382★	101	9009★	1213★
367	5020	216★	605	2155	50★	782	6230	308	912	5465	205	3022	—	8581★	102	—	1208★
368	5005★	240★	606	7260	335	783	6220★	307	913	5460★	209	3023	—	8581★	103	—	1210★
369	5005	213★	608	7255	333★	791	4165★	941★	915	3030	89★	3024	1100	900★	104	9012	1217
370	—	889★	610	5825T	889★	792	4155T	940	917	3020★	89★	3031	—	905★	105	9013★	1218
371	—	888★	611	5735T	898	793	4155	121	918	8330★	341★	3032	8620T	903★	106	9002T	1203★
372	—	887★	612	8815★	832	794	4145	120★	919	8095★	341★	3033	8610★	388★	107	9003	1204
400	8325★	351	613	5605★	956★	796	4340	133★	920	8060★	339★	3041	3215★	871	108	9014★	1220★
402	8305★	347★	632	8530	936★	797	4265★	132★	921	8060T	349★	3042	3205★	869	111	—	1218★
407	8005	882★	640	8625	903	798	4325	131★	922	8315T	324★	3045	6260T	373★	112	9003T	1204★
413	1025★	401	642	8620★	392	799	4250★	130★	924	4830T	851★	3046	5810	887★	113	9007★	1210★
414	1020★	400★	644	8800	830	800	4310	128	926	4820★	779★	3047	5805	886★	114	9010	1215
415	1015	398	645	1115	905★	801	8405	357★	927	4810T	849★	3051	5530T	846★	115	9004	1206
420	8720★	375★	646	1115★	8581	806	4870T	169★	928	1010T	900★	3052	5060★	859★	121	9007	1210
422	8710★	373★	647	1110	8581★	807	4860★	168★	930	4510	922★	3053	5055★	859★	122	9010T	1215★
433	8265	371★	648	1100★	900	809	4145★	130★	931	4505	921★	3064	8005★	914★	123	—	1213★
434	8215★	309	666	2405	46	813	4610★	160★	932	4500	920★	3072	4805★	397★	124	9007T	1210★
435	8210★	369★	676	6250	891	814	2340T	44★	934	5070T	862★	3078	6130	292★	125	9009	1213
436	8205	363★	677	—	886★	815	2530★	43	935	5225T	862★	3325	4200	159★	126	9006★	1208★

2

Designs Inspired by
Historic Works of Art

PRIMITIVE CATTLE

(Based on a cave painting from the Sahara, about 3500 BC)

Material: beige linen, 8 threads per cm (20 threads per in)
Design size: 38 × 56 cm (15 × 22 in)
Thread: DMC embroidery floss. Use 3 strands in the needle

◣ 898 darkest brown

◪ 300 dark brown

☒ 975 medium brown

▥ 436 light brown

⊡ 437 lightest brown

CUSHION WITH LIONS

(Based on a detail from King Nebuchadnezzar's royal chamber, Babylon, 6th century BC)

Material: medium blue burlap, 6 threads per cm (15 threads per in)
Cutting size: 50 × 55 cm (19½ × 21½ in)
Finished size: 44 × 47 cm (17¼ × 18½ in)
Thread: DMC embroidery floss. Use 4 strands in the needle

■ 310 black
⊠ 721 orange
Ḻ 822 cream
⊡ 827 light blue
◣ 632 dark brown

◪ 407 medium brown
Ⅲ 950 light brown

CURTAIN WITH WILD GEESE

(Based on a Japanese design, 18th century)

Material: beige linen, 8 threads per cm (20 threads per in)
Cutting size: 55 cm (21½ in) deep × length required
Thread: DMC embroidery floss. Use 4 strands in the needle

The charts for this project continue on pages 22 and 23.

⊡	319 dark green
⊠	988 medium green
𝖼	471 light green
◤	310 black
◿	3024 grey
⫿	762 light grey
◹	white

Before starting work, plan out how the geese should be placed along the curtain so that you avoid ending with only a portion of a goose. Begin to embroider 7 cm (2¾ in) from the lower edge. Finish with a 2 cm (¾ in) hem on the bottom and a 1 cm (½ in) hem on the other sides.

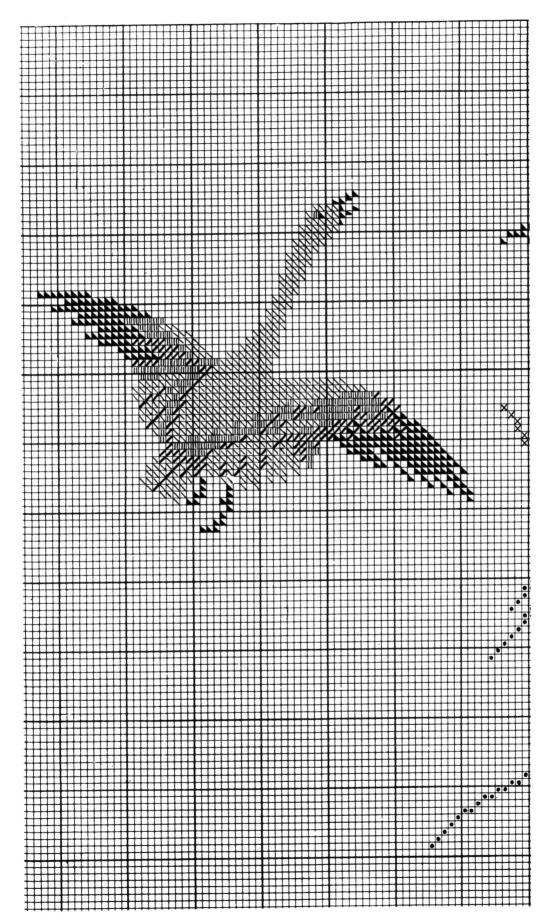

SEAT COVER WITH COCKERELS
(Based on a traditional Polish paper collage design, 17th century)

Material: Aida, $4\frac{1}{2}$ stitches per cm (11 stitches per in)
Cutting size: 42×42 cm ($16\frac{1}{2} \times 16\frac{1}{2}$ in)
Finished size: 35×35 cm ($13\frac{3}{4} \times 13\frac{3}{4}$ in)
Circular foam rubber pad: 35 cm ($13\frac{3}{4}$ in) diameter
Zipper: 30 cm ($11\frac{3}{4}$ in)
Bias tape: 120 cm (47 in)
Thread: DMC embroidery floss. Use 3 strands in the needle

- ● 310 black
- ③ 783 gold
- ⸱ 733 olive
- ◪ 3348 light green
- ◣ 815 dark red
- ⊘ 350 medium red
- ⊟ 352 light red
- · 758 lightest salmon

Sew lengths of bias tape to the edge of the completed seat cover so that it may be tied to a chair.

CUSHION WITH BIRDS

(Based on a traditional Polish paper collage design, 17th century)

Material: Aida, 5½ stitches per cm (13½ stitches per in)
Cutting size: 38 × 38 cm (15 × 15 in)
Finished size: 31 × 31 cm (12¼ × 12¼ in)
Zipper: about 30 cm (11¾ in)
Thread: DMC embroidery floss. Use 2 strands in the needle

3	797 blue	⊘	971 orange
◣	550 lilac	C	972 yellow
Y	917 cyclamen	☒	350 red
V	899 rose	●	310 black
·	353 light salmon		
⊠	906 green		

HORSE

*(Based on a drawing by
Leonardo da Vinci, 1452–1519)*

Material: beige Aida, 5 stitches per
cm (13 stitches per in)
Design size: 17.5 × 15.5 cm
($6\frac{3}{4}$ × 6 in)
Thread: DMC embroidery floss. Use
2 strands in the needle

◧ 898 dark brown

◪ 433 medium brown

⊠ 435 light brown

⊡ 3023 grey

3

Domestic and Wild Animals

Wallhanging with chickens (spring)

Material: linen, 10 threads per cm
(25 threads per in)
Cutting size: 36 × 40 cm
(14 × 15¾ in)
Finished size: 26 × 30.5 cm
(10¼ × 12 in)
Piece of cardboard: 26 × 30.5 cm
(10¼ × 12 in)
Thread: DMC embroidery floss. Use
2 strands in the needle

⊓	986 dark green
⊟	988 medium green
⋀	907 light green
⊙	210 lilac
⊞	371 beige
◣	310 black
◪	300 dark rust
⊡	920 medium rust
⊠	922 light rust
⌊	977 gold
◩	725 yellow
⸦	350 red
⟍	947 orange

To finish, count 9 threads from the
border and fold the fabric under all
round to make a neat edge. Glue in
place on the cardboard.

WALLHANGING WITH COW (SUMMER)

Material: linen, 10 threads per cm
(25 threads per in)
Cutting size: 36 × 40 cm
(14 × 15¾ in)
Finished size: 26 × 30.5 cm
(10¼ × 12 in)
Piece of cardboard: 26 × 30.5 cm
(10¼ × 12 in)
Thread: DMC embroidery floss. Use
2 strands in the needle

⊞	904	dark green
☒	470	medium green
⊡	471	light green
◣	838	dark brown
◪	420	light brown
⊡	970	dark orange
◯	741	light orange
⊙	400	darkest rust
⊪	976	dark rust
⋀	402	medium rust
⊟	738	light rust

To finish, count 9 threads from the
border and fold the fabric under all
round to make a neat edge. Glue in
place on the cardboard.

WALLHANGING WITH GOATS (AUTUMN)

Material: linen, 10 threads per cm
(25 threads per in)
Cutting size: 36 × 40 cm
(14 × 15¾ in)
Finished size: 26 × 30.5 cm
(10¼ × 12 in)
Piece of cardboard: 26 × 30.5 cm
(10¼ × 12 in)
Thread: DMC embroidery floss. Use
2 strands in the needle

◤ 310 black

◪ 3371 darkest brown

▥ 3781 dark brown

∧ 420 medium brown

L 3045 light brown

⊙ 350 red

⊠ 470 green

◩ 733 dull green

⊐ 725 yellow

⊞ 680 gold

⊙ 976 rust

◥ 402 light rust

To finish, count 9 threads from the
border and fold the fabric under all
round to make a neat edge. Glue in
place on the cardboard.

Wallhanging with owl and fox (winter)

Material: linen, 10 threads per cm
(25 threads per in)
Cutting size: 36 × 40 cm
(14 × 15¾ in)
Finished size: 26 × 30.5 cm
(10¼ × 12 in)
Piece of cardboard: 26 × 30.5 cm
(10¼ × 12 in)
Thread: DMC embroidery floss. Use
2 strands in the needle

■ 310 black

▨ 3022 grey

◣ 935 very dark green

☒ 470 light green

⊙ 433 brown

▥ 680 gold

⊟ 738 beige

⊠ 740 orange

◥ 921 dark rust

ㄴ 922 light rust

◎ 799 blue

To finish, count 9 threads from the
border and fold the fabric under all
round to make a neat edge. Glue in
place on the cardboard.

SQUIRREL

Material: linen, 10 threads per cm
(25 threads per in)
Design size: 13 × 15.5 cm (5 × 6 in)
Thread: DMC embroidery floss. Use
2 strands in the needle

■ 310 black

◣ 975 darkest brown

◪ 301 dark brown

◺ 3776 medium brown

⊓ 402 light brown

⊡ 3011 dark grey-green

⊟ 831 dull green

L 733 light yellowish green

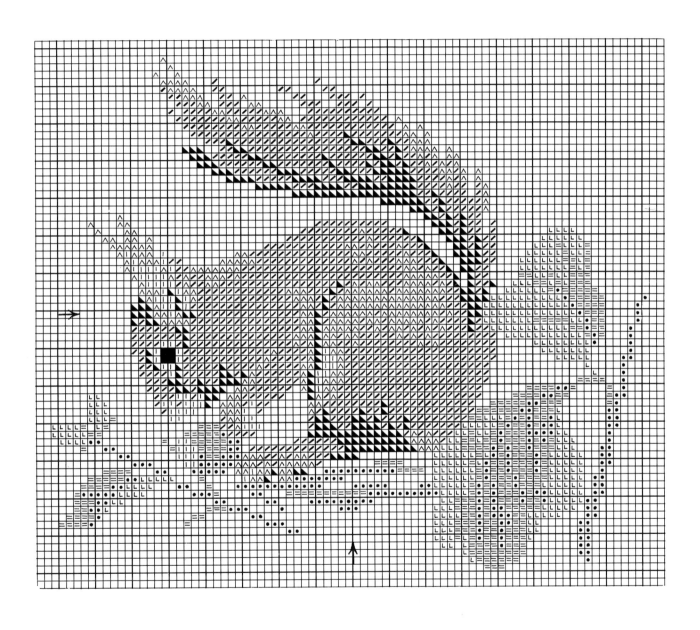

WALLHANGING WITH CAT IN A CHERRY TREE

Material: linen, 8 threads per cm
(20 threads per in)
Cutting size: 35 × 40 cm
(13¾ × 15¾ in)
Finished size: 28 × 33 cm (11 × 13 in)
Fitting
Thread: DMC embroidery floss. Use
3 strands in the needle

- ⊙ 975 reddish brown
- ⧄ 3776 rust
- ⌃ 402 light rust
- ⭦ 738 beige
- ⊡ 712 light beige
- ⊓ 937 dark green
- ⊠ 470 medium green
- ∟ 581 light green
- ⊟ 734 lightest green
- ■ 310 black
- ◣ 839 dark brown
- ⊜ 840 light brown
- ⊓ 725 yellow
- ⧄ 814 dark red
- ⧄ 347 red

The mouth is backstitched with 975,
the whiskers with 738 and reflected
light in the eyes with 712.

WALLHANGING WITH CAT AND FLOWERS

Material: linen, 8 threads per cm (20 threads per in)
Cutting size: 42 × 52 cm ($16\frac{1}{2} \times 20\frac{1}{2}$ in)
Finished size: 39 × 49 cm ($15\frac{1}{2} \times 19\frac{1}{4}$ in)
Bias binding: 185 cm (73 in)
Thread: DMC embroidery floss. Use 3 strands in the needle

- ◣ 3021 dark brown
- ▨ 611 medium brown
- L 613 dark beige
- ⧅ 822 light beige
- ⊟ 580 dark yellowish green
- ∧ 581 light yellowish green
- ⊡ 986 darkest green
- ╫ 905 dark green
- ⊠ 906 medium green
- ⁄ 704 light green
- O 407 reddish brown
- ⊞ 3708 rose
- S 742 orange
- ↗ 726 yellow

The whiskers are backstitched with 613 and the outlines of the eyes with 3021. After ironing the finished embroidery, sew bias binding around the edges.

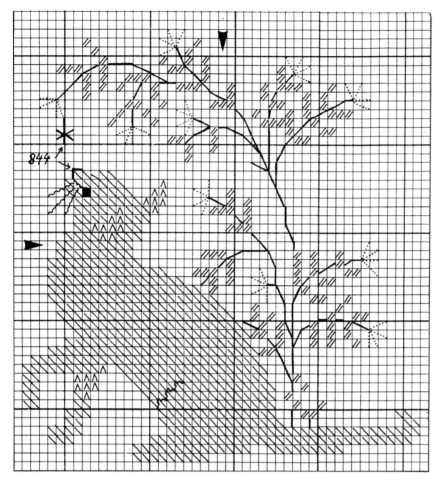

PLATE LINER WITH CAT AND BLUE FLOWERS

Material: beige linen, 8 threads per cm (20 threads per in)
Cutting size: 20×20 cm (8×8 in)
Finished size: 16×16 cm ($6\frac{1}{4} \times 6\frac{1}{4}$ in)
Thread: DMC embroidery floss and pearl yarn no. 5. Use 4 strands in the needle and 1 strand of pearl yarn

```
····  798 blue (backstitch)
```

☑ 580 green

— 580 (backstitch)

■ 844 dark grey

⋀ 415 light grey

∼∼ 415 (backstitch)

◻ white (pearl yarn no. 5)

Hem the embroidery with tiny hem stitches sewn with white pearl yarn.

PLATE LINER WITH CAT AND RED FLOWERS

Material: beige linen, 8 threads per cm (20 threads per in)
Cutting size: 20 × 20 cm (8 × 8 in)
Finished size: 16 × 16 cm (6¼ × 6¼ in)
Thread: DMC embroidery floss and pearl yarn no. 5. Use 4 strands in the needle and 1 strand of pearl yarn

- ■ 335 red
- ▨ 580 green
- ⊡ 907 light green (eyes)
- — 844 dark grey (eyes)
- — 414 medium grey (backstitch for nose, mouth)
- ⋀ 415 light grey
- ◺ white (pearl yarn no. 5)

The whiskers on the right are backstitched with 415; those on the left in white. The stems of the flowers are backstitched with 580. Finish the plate liner as described on the opposite page.

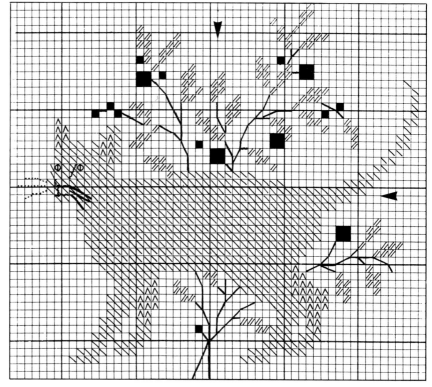

PLATE LINER WITH CAT AND YELLOW FLOWERS

Material: beige linen, 8 threads per cm (20 threads per in)
Cutting size: 20 × 20 cm (8 × 8 in)
Finished size: 16 × 16 cm (6¼ × 6¼ in)
Thread: DMC embroidery floss and pearl yarn no. 5. Use 4 strands in the needle and 1 strand of pearl yarn

- ⬤ 783 dark yellow
- L 725 light yellow
- ▨ 580 green
- — 580 (backstitch)
- ⦂ 907 light green (eye)
- ⫿ 844 dark grey (eye)
- ∧ 415 light grey
- ∼ 415 (backstitch)
- ◻ white (pearl yarn no. 5)

The whiskers and outline of a front 'elbow' are backstitched with 415. Finish the plate liner as described on page 44.

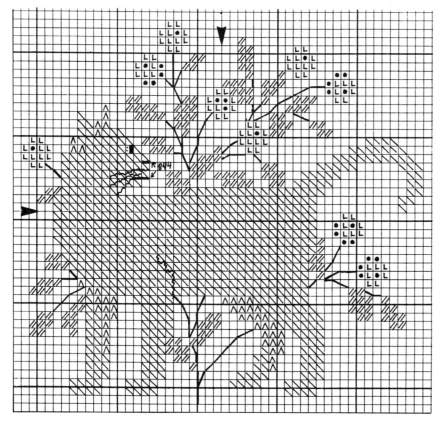

PLATE LINER WITH CAT AND LILAC FLOWERS

Material: beige linen, 8 threads per cm (20 threads per in)
Cutting size: 20 × 20 cm (8 × 8 in)
Finished size: 16 × 16 cm (6¼ × 6¼ in)
Thread: DMC embroidery floss and pearl yarn no. 5. Use 4 strands in the needle and 1 strand of pearl yarn

◣ 327 lilac

▨ 580 green

— 580 (backstitch)

⊙ 725 yellow (eyes)

■ 844 dark grey

⋀ 415 light grey

〜 415 (backstitch)

▢ white (pearl yarn no. 5)

The whiskers and outline of a front 'elbow' and back leg are backstitched with 415. The pupils of the eyes, and the mouth are sewn with 844. Finish the plate liner as described on page 44.

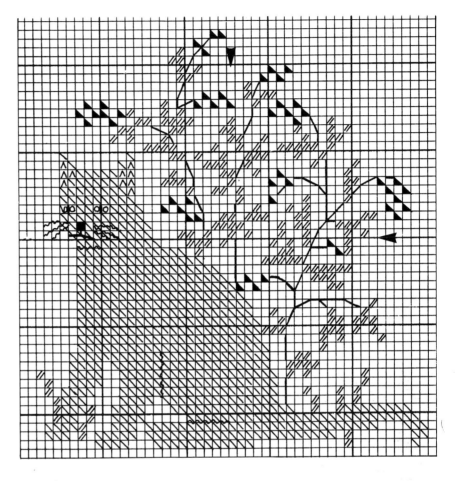

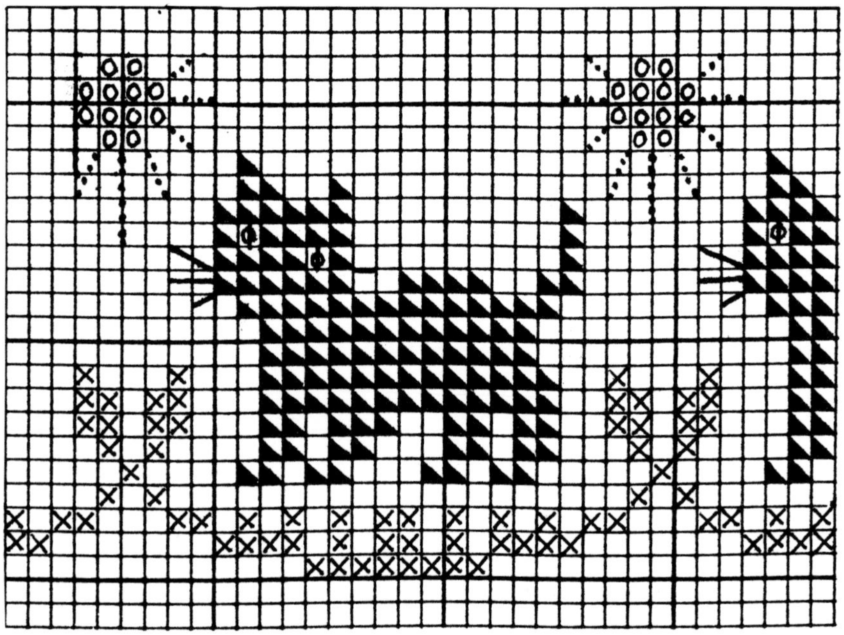

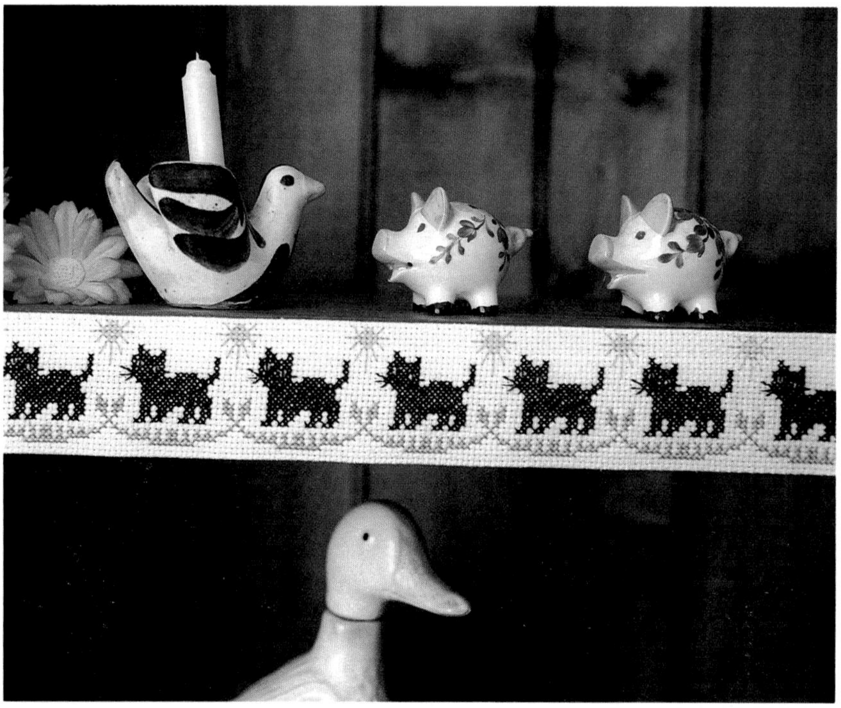

Decorative border with cats

Material: Aida, $5\frac{1}{2}$ stitches per cm ($13\frac{1}{2}$ stitches per in)
Cutting size: 8 cm (3 in) × length required
Thread: DMC embroidery floss. Use 2 strands in the needle

- ◣ 310 black
- — 310 (backstitch)
- ☒ 907 green
- ◎ 972 yellow
- ····· 972 (backstitch)

Iron the finished embroidery and fold over the long sides to make a small hem. The border may be sewn on to a towel or attached to a shelf.

SPECTACLE CASE
WITH DOGS

Material: linen, 10 threads per cm
(25 threads per in)
Cutting size: front 12×20 cm
($4\frac{3}{4} \times 8$ in); back 5 cm (2 in) longer or
more, depending on the length of
your spectacles
Finished size: 9×16 cm ($3\frac{1}{2} \times 6\frac{1}{4}$ in)
2 pieces of interfacing: sizes as
cutting size for front and back
2 pieces of backing material: sizes
as cutting size for front and back
Cord: 80 cm ($31\frac{1}{2}$ in)
Thread: DMC embroidery floss. Use
2 strands in the needle

■	830	brown
∧	335	red
∧	553	lilac
∧	798	blue
∧	906	green
●	977	gold

(dogs) — brackets grouping 335 red, 553 lilac, 798 blue, 906 green

Iron the finished embroidery and
turn under a small hem all round.
With the embroidered side face
down, lay the interfacing and then
the backing material on the linen.
Cut away the surplus fabric. Turn
under the edges of the backing
material and sew it to the linen with
small stitches. Sew the front and back
of the spectacle case together and sew
on the cord.

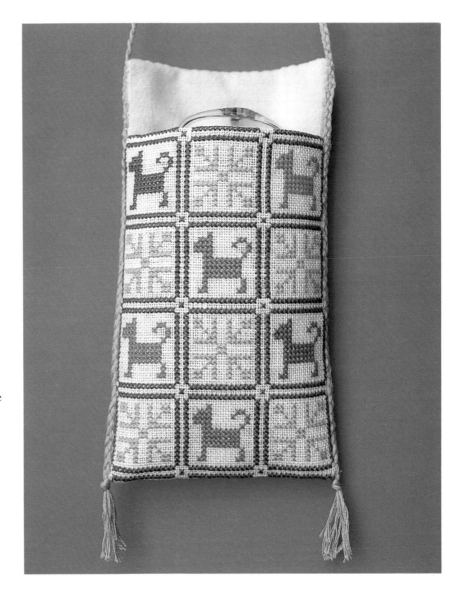

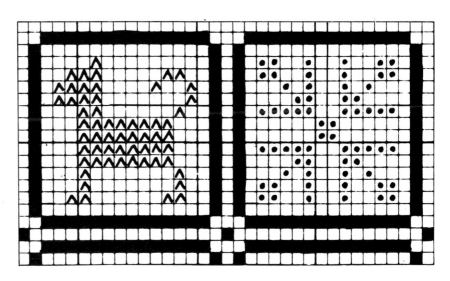

BOOKMARK WITH DOGS

Material: linen, 10 threads per cm
(25 threads per in)
Cutting size: 20 × 8 cm (8 × 3 in)
Finished size: 20 × 3.5 cm (8 × 1½ in)
Thread: DMC embroidery floss. Use
2 strands in the needle

— 830 brown (backstitch)

☒ 335 red ⎫
☒ 553 lilac ⎪
☒ 798 blue ⎬ (dogs)
☒ 906 green ⎭

Iron the finished embroidery. Fold
the long edges to the wrong side,
overlap slightly and stitch neatly in
place. Make a fringe of about 2 cm
(¾ in) at the top and bottom by
removing threads.

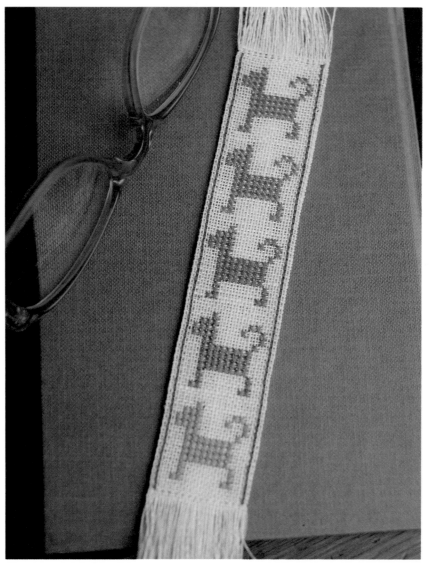

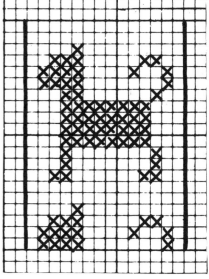

JUMPING
KANGAROOS

Material: linen, 10 threads per cm
(25 threads per in)
Design size: 14×11 cm ($5\frac{1}{2} \times 4\frac{1}{4}$ in)
Thread: DMC embroidery floss. Use
2 strands in the needle

⊠ 434 brown

◣ 320 green

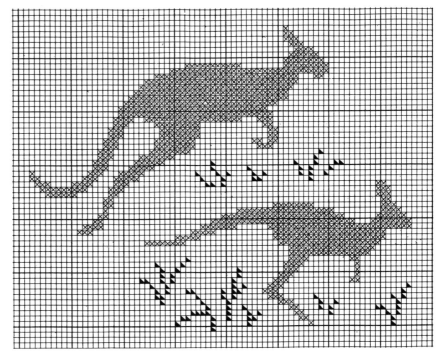

KANGAROO WITH BABY IN POUCH

Material: linen, 10 threads per cm (25 threads per in)
Design size: 15 × 21 cm (5¾ × 8¼ in)
Thread: DMC embroidery floss. Use 2 strands in the needle

◣ 3021 darkest brown

◪ 434 dark brown

⋀ 436 medium brown

ⳑ 738 light brown

◉ 937 dark green

⬓ 470 light green

CUSHION WITH REINDEER

Material: linen, 8 threads per cm
(20 threads per in)
Cutting size: 45 × 45 cm
(17¾ × 17¾ in)
Finished size: about 39 × 39 cm
(15½ × 15½ in)
Zipper: 30 cm (11¾ in)
Thread: DMC embroidery floss. Use
3 strands in the needle

■	310 black
◣	3781 dark brown
⧄	3790 brown
ٯ	642 dark beige
◩	3782 medium beige
L	3033 light beige

⊠	988 green
⊙	869 golden-brown
⧄	3045 gold
⊙	827 light blue

KOALA BEAR

Material: linen, 10 threads per cm
(25 threads per in)
Design size: 10.5 × 11.5 cm
(4 × 4½ in)
Thread: DMC embroidery floss. Use
2 strands in the needle

▇ 310 black

◣ 535 darkest grey

▨ 646 dark grey

☒ 647 medium grey

ⓛ 3024 light grey

⊡ 3790 brown

◩ 612 dark beige

▨ 644 light beige

▥ 320 green

◩ 368 light green

ⓒ 471 light yellowish green

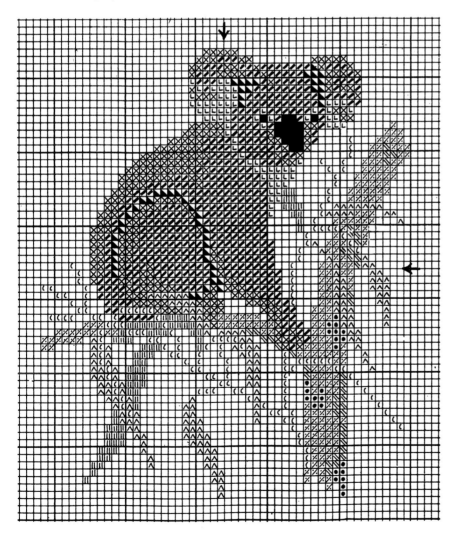

GIBBON AMONG BRANCHES

Material: linen, 10 threads per cm (25 threads per in)
Design size: 10.5 × 16 cm (4 × 6¼ in)
Thread: DMC embroidery floss. Use 2 strands in the needle

◣ 310 black

◿ 844 dark grey

◭ 646 medium grey

◫ 644 light grey

● 611 brown

◺ 904 dark green

L 906 medium green

◿ 907 light green

BABY ELEPHANT

Material: linen, 10 threads per cm
(25 threads per in)
Design size: 15.5 × 14 cm (6 × 5½ in)
Thread: DMC embroidery floss. Use
2 strands in the needle

■ 310 black

◩ 3021 dark brown

◪ 610 medium brown

⊞ 611 light brown

L 612 lightest brown

☒ 581 green

PANDA

Material: beige linen, 8 threads per cm (20 threads per in)
Design size: 14×9 cm ($5\frac{1}{2} \times 3\frac{1}{2}$ in)
Thread: DMC embroidery floss. Use 3 strands in the needle

◥ 310 black

— 310 (backstitch)

Ⓛ white

Ⅲ 831 brown

☒ 906 green

◎ 907 light green

--- 907 (backstitch)

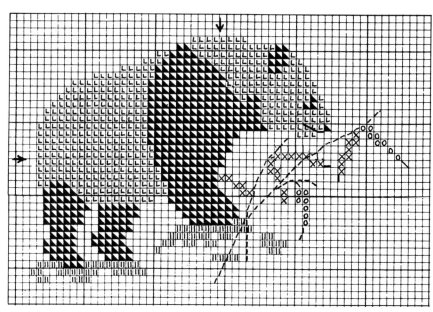

4

Birds

BLUE TIT BORDER FOR TOWEL

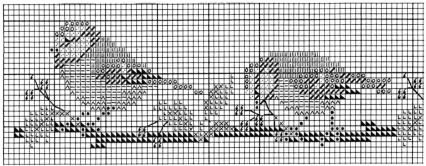

Material: linen, 10 threads per cm (25 threads per in)
Cutting size: 8 cm (3 in) × width of towel
Thread: DMC embroidery floss. Use 2 strands in the needle

⊠	906 green
—	906 (backstitch)
Ⓛ	907 light green
⸢	347 red
◣	844 dark grey
⊠	930 dark dull blue

⫼	502 light blue-green
Ⓞ	799 blue
⊡	white
●	611 light brown
⋀	734 gold
⊟	3047 light gold

Iron the finished embroidery and fold under the long sides to make a small hem. Machine-stitch the border to the towel.

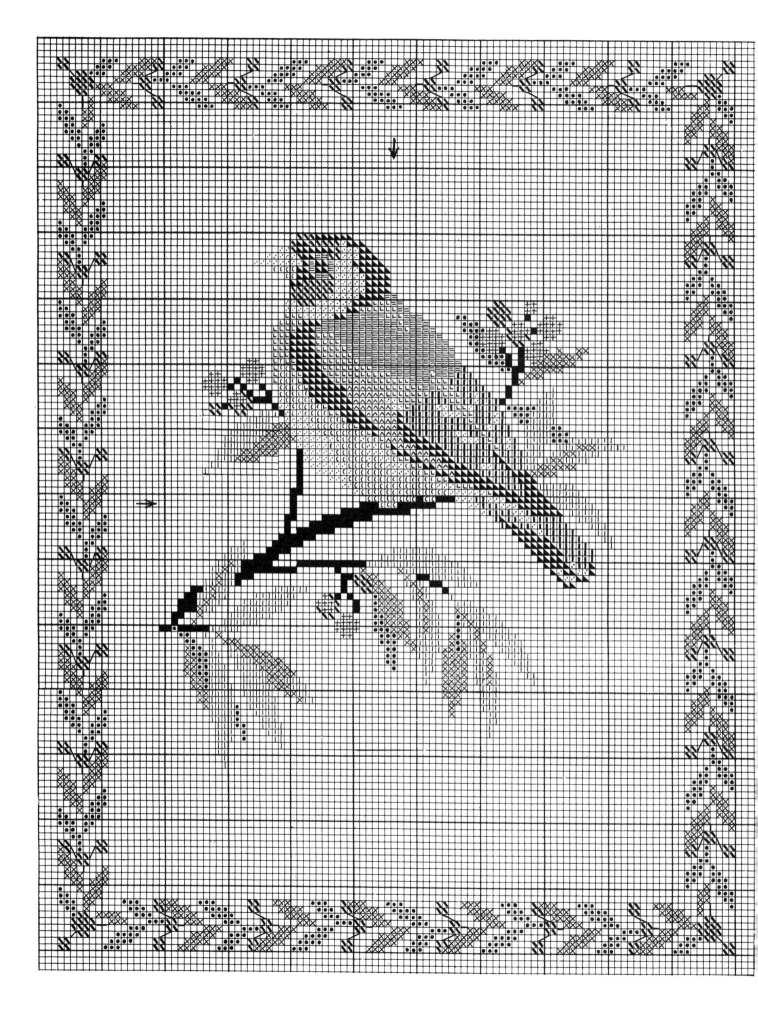

WALLHANGING WITH GOLDFINCH

Material: linen, 10 threads per cm
(25 threads per in)
Cutting size: 28 × 34 cm
(11 × 13½ in)
Finished size: 20.5 × 26.5 cm
(8 × 10½ in)
Piece of cardboard: 20.5 × 26.5 cm
(8 × 10½ in)
Thread: DMC embroidery floss. Use
2 strands in the needle

⊙	501	dark blue-green
⊠	988	medium green
—	988	(backstitch)
⊞	471	light green
◣	3371	darkest brown
⫿	3781	dark brown
⊟	420	medium brown
⌊	3045	light brown
⟮	613	beige
⫶	3033	light beige
■	731	dull green
◥	347	dark red
⊞	900	red
⌃	743	yellow

Count 16 threads from the border
and fold the fabric under all round to
make a neat edge. Glue in place on
the cardboard.

CUSHION WITH REDSTART

Material: linen, 8 threads per cm (20 threads per in)

Cutting size: 40 × 45 cm (15¾ × 17¾ in)

Finished size: 35 × 40 cm (13¾ × 15¾ in)

Zipper: 30 cm (11¾ in)

Thread: DMC embroidery floss. Use 3 strands in the needle

∕	3345 darkest green		K	317 dark grey
⊞	3346 dark green		∧	414 medium grey
✕	470 medium green		∙	762 light grey
L	471 light green		▬	921 dark rust
◣	310 black		⊙	922 medium rust
●	610 greyish brown		↗	402 light rust
‖	612 beige		⊓	738 light beige

CUSHION WITH ICTERINE WARBLER

Material: linen, 8 threads per cm
(20 threads per in)
Cutting size: 40 × 45 cm
($15\frac{3}{4}$ × $17\frac{3}{4}$ in)
Finished size: 35 × 40 cm
($13\frac{3}{4}$ × $15\frac{3}{4}$ in)
Zipper: 30 cm ($11\frac{3}{4}$ in)
Thread: DMC embroidery floss. Use
3 strands in the needle

◩ 3345 darkest green

⊞ 3346 dark green

☒ 470 medium green

L 471 light green

◣ 310 black

⊡ 3781 brown

Ⅲ 611 darkest beige

∧ 371 beige

◙ 834 gold

↗ 444 bright yellow

Ⅱ 726 light yellow

LAPWING

Material: linen, 10 threads per cm (25 threads per in)
Design size: 11 × 12 cm (4¼ × 4¾ in)
Thread: DMC embroidery floss. Use 2 strands in the needle

◣ 319 dark blue-green

◪ 580 green

⊠ 470 light green

Ⅼ 471 lightest green

◉ 434 brown

⋀ 680 light brown

Ⅲ 733 yellowish green

⊟ 734 light yellowish green

■ 310 black

⊂ 415 grey

·. white

◎ 3716 rose

CHRISTMAS CARD WITH ROBIN

Material: linen, 10 threads per cm (25 threads per in)
Cutting size: 16×20 cm ($6\frac{1}{4} \times 8$ in)
Finished size: $11\frac{1}{2} \times 16$ cm ($4\frac{1}{2} \times 6\frac{1}{4}$ in)
Piece of thin card: about 27×18 cm ($10\frac{3}{4} \times 7$ in)
Coloured paper
Thread: DMC embroidery floss and gold metallic thread. Use 2 strands in the needle and 1 strand of gold metallic thread.

■ 310 black

⊞ 414 grey

◢ 648 light grey

◉ 610 brown

◩ 611 dark beige

⋅ 644 light beige

K 921 dark rust

O 922 light rust

◣ 986 darkest green

◿ 988 dark green

∧ 3347 medium green

L 472 light green

⊟ 349 red

— 349 (backstitch)

⊠ gold metallic thread

Iron the finished embroidery and carefully trim 2 cm ($\frac{3}{4}$ in) from all round the edge of the fabric. Fold the card in half. Using transparent glue, glue the embroidery to the 'front' of the card. Cut a mount from the coloured paper, with inner measurements the same as those of the embroidery, and glue it in place on the front of the card.

BLUE TIT

Material: linen, 8 threads per cm (20 threads per in)
Design size: 26×30 cm
($10\frac{1}{4} \times 11\frac{3}{4}$ in)
Thread: DMC embroidery floss. Use 3 strands in the needle

■ 310 black

◣ 336 darkest blue

◪ 312 dark blue

Ⓞ 334 medium blue

⊟ 3325 light blue

Ⓢ 647 grey

Ⓛ 762 light grey

∴ white

⫴ 3052 grey-green

∧ 3053 light green

⧄ 676 gold

⧄ 726 light yellow

◸ 610 brown

● 899 dark rose

⊠ 776 medium rose

Ⅲ 818 light rose

⊟ 3346 dark green

⊞ 3347 medium green

⧄ 471 light green

EASTER PLACEMAT I

Material: linen, 8 threads per cm
(20 threads per in)
Cutting size: 40 × 50 cm
($15\frac{3}{4} \times 19\frac{1}{2}$ in)
Finished size: 34 × 44 cm
($13\frac{1}{2} \times 17\frac{1}{4}$ in)
Thread: DMC embroidery floss. Use
3 strands in the needle

◣ 367 dark green

◿ 906 medium green

☒ 907 light green

⊡ 733 dark dull green

⊙ 734 light dull green

Ⅱ 721 dark orange

◺ 972 light orange

～ 972 (backstitch)

Ⅼ 444 yellow

— 444 (backstitch)

⊟ 307 light yellow

■ 310 black

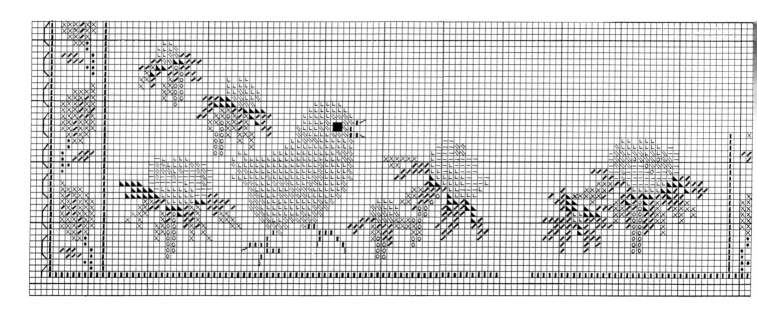

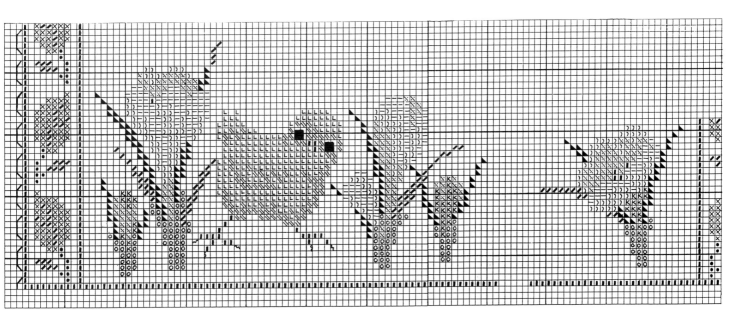

EASTER PLACEMAT II

Material: linen, 8 threads per cm
(20 threads per in)
Cutting size: 40 × 50 cm
(15¾ × 19½ in)
Finished size: 34 × 44 cm
(13½ × 17¼ in)
Thread: DMC embroidery floss. Use
3 strands in the needle

◣ 367 dark green

◪ 906 medium green

⊠ 907 light green

◉ 733 dark dull green

◎ 734 light dull green

Ḱ 552 dark lilac

◩ 553 medium lilac

⊐ 210 light lilac

⊟ 211 lightest lilac

⫿ 721 dark orange

⁓ 721 (backstitch)

◺ 972 light orange

— 972 (backstitch)

⊡ 444 yellow

■ 310 black

Egg cosies

Material: linen, 10 threads per cm
(25 threads per in)
Cutting size: (2 pieces) 10 × 12 cm
(3¾ × 4¾ in)
Foam insulation
Cord: 25 cm (9¾ in)
Thread: DMC embroidery floss. Use
2 strands in the needle

●	906 dark green
∼	906 (backstitch)
✕	907 light green
◣	552 dark lilac
▨	553 light lilac
◲	721 dark orange

—	721 (backstitch)
∧	741 medium orange
▧	725 light orange
■	310 black

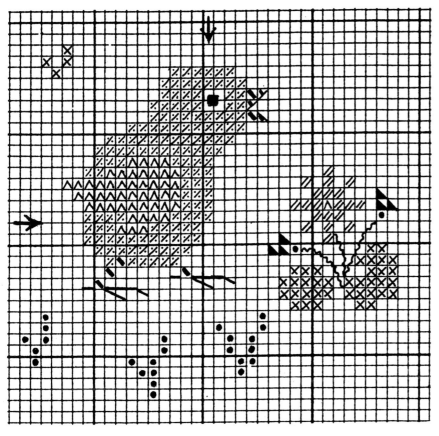

Cut 2 layers of linen and 2 layers of foam insulation using the diagram opposite as a pattern. Embroider the design on the linen. With right sides facing, place the 2 pieces of linen together and sandwich them between the 2 pieces of foam. Stitch around the curved edge, leaving the straight side open. Trim away the surplus material ½ cm (¼ in) from the curved seam and 2 cm (¾ in) from the open edge. Turn up the open edge and sew with small stitches to the foam insulation. Turn the right side out and stitch on the cord.

MATCHBOX COVER WITH SEAGULL

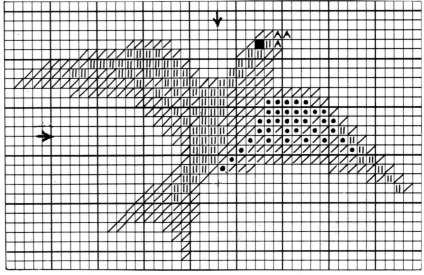

Material: blue Aida, $4\frac{1}{2}$ stitches per cm (11 stitches per in)
Cutting size: 15×10 cm ($6\frac{3}{4} \times 3\frac{3}{4}$ in)
Piece of cardboard: same size as top of matchbox
Thread: DMC embroidery floss. Use 3 strands in the needle

Iron the finished embroidery. Place it face down, lay the cardboard in the centre, turn up the edges of the linen and glue them to the cardboard. Put some glue on the surface of the matchbox and press on the embroidery-covered cardboard.

●	318 grey
▥	415 light grey
◹	white
■	898 brown
⋀	725 yellow

BIRDS ON THE WIRE

Material: Aida, 7¾ stitches per cm
(19 stitches per in)
Design size: 10 × 8.5 cm (3¾ × 3¼ in)

Thread: DMC embroidery floss. Use
2 strands in the needle

◤ 311 blue

▥ 414 grey

PENGUINS

Material: linen, 10 threads per cm
(25 threads per in)
Design size: 18×10 cm ($7 \times 3\frac{3}{4}$ in)
Thread: DMC embroidery floss. Use
2 strands in the needle

◣ 310 black

◪ 844 dark grey

◉ 647 light grey

⊟ white

⊞ 407 beige

GREY CARDINAL

Material: Aida, 5½ stitches per cm
(13½ stitches per in)
Design size: 12 × 12 cm (4¾ × 4¾ in)
Thread: DMC embroidery floss. Use
2 strands in the needle

⧄	905 dark green
⫼	906 medium green
⊠	907 light green
⊟	347 dark red
⊞	350 red
⊙	922 light rust
◼	310 black

◣	535 dark grey
⊠	451 medium grey
⊟	452 light grey
⬘	3782 dark beige
⫶	712 ecru
⊙	3045 light brown

WALLHANGING WITH PARROT

Material: linen, 10 threads per cm
(25 threads per in)
Cutting size: 23×35 cm ($9 \times 13\frac{3}{4}$ in)
Finished size: 18×28 cm (7×11 in)
Fitting
Thread: DMC embroidery floss. Use
2 strands in the needle

◣ 535 darkest grey

⌜⌐⌝ 3022 medium grey

К 648 light grey

◨ 3790 brown

L 3033 beige

⊟ 517 dark blue

⊠ 807 medium blue

⊡ 519 light blue

■ 309 dark red

⊤ 891 bright red

⊙ 988 dark green

▧ 702 medium green

◻ 703 light green

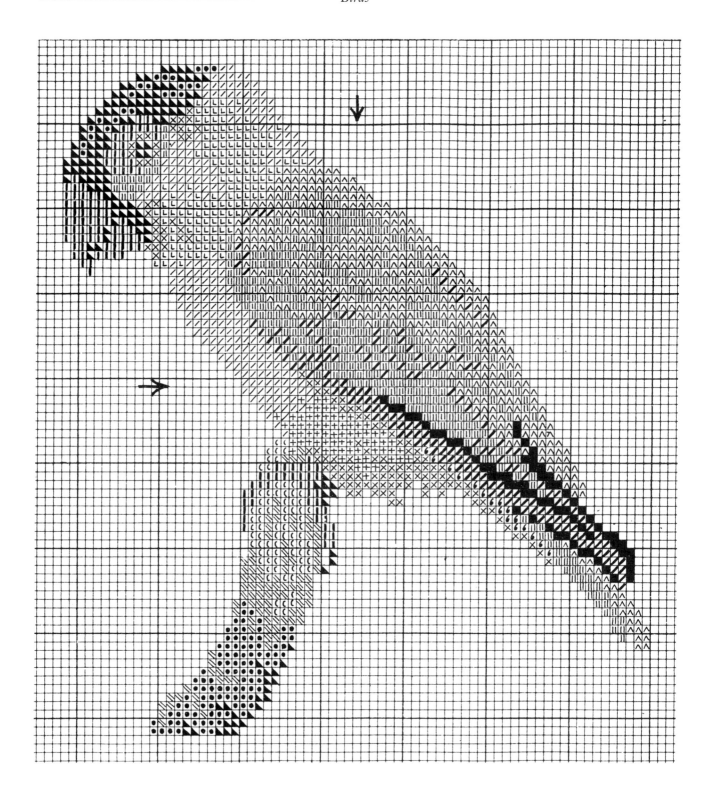

PARAKEET

Material: linen, 8 threads per cm
(20 threads per in)
Design size: 18 × 20 cm (7 × 8 in)
Thread: DMC embroidery floss. Use
3 strands in the needle

◥ 3021 darkest brown

⊡ 640 grey-brown

◲ 841 reddish beige

⊂ 3782 light reddish beige

◫ 3022 grey

■ 934 darkest green

◨ 3362 dark green

Ⅱ 988 medium green

⋀ 906 light green

˪ 782 dark gold

⊠ 977 medium gold

⊞ 725 yellow

˪ 444 bright yellow

◿ 744 light yellow

IMPERIAL EAGLE

Material: linen, 10 threads per cm   ☒ 310 black
(25 threads per in)
Design size: 10.5 × 13 cm (4 × 5 in)
Thread: DMC embroidery floss. Use
2 strands in the needle

WALLHANGING OR TABLE RUNNER WITH BIRDS

Material: linen, 8 threads per cm
(20 threads per in)
Cutting size: 25 × 100 cm
($9\frac{3}{4} \times 39\frac{1}{2}$ in)
Finished size: 18 × 90 cm ($7 \times 35\frac{1}{2}$ in)
Thread: DMC pearl cotton no. 5

⊠ 518 turquoise

— 518 (backstitch)

⦿ 310 black

〰 310 (backstitch)

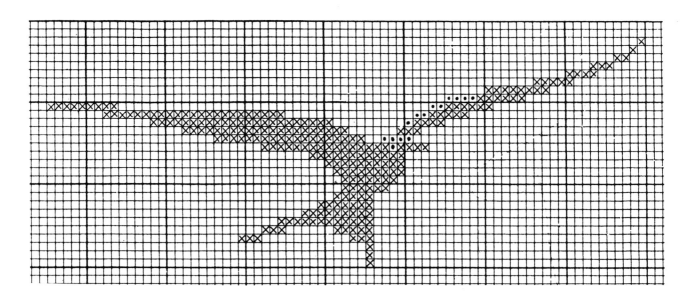

Flying bird

Material: linen, 10 threads per cm
(25 threads per in)
Design size: 14.5 × 5 cm (5½ × 2 in)

Thread: DMC embroidery floss. Use
2 strands in the needle

☒ 311 dark blue
⦿ 318 grey

5

Insects and Butterflies

SPIDER IN ITS WEB

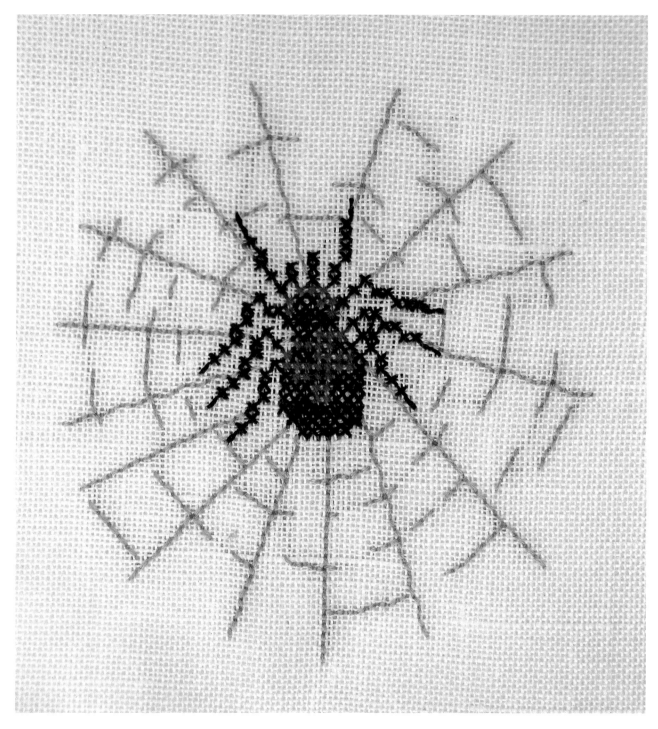

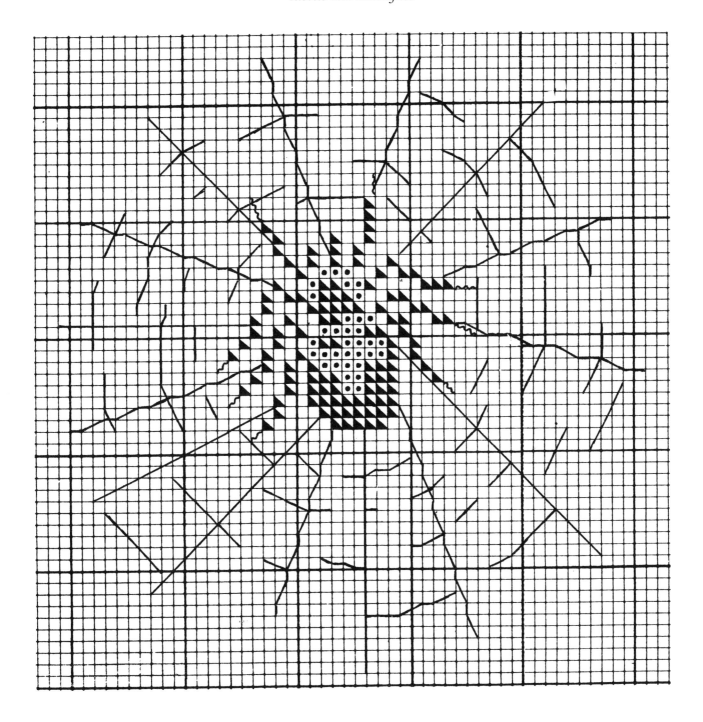

Material: linen, 10 threads per cm
(25 threads per in)
Design size: 10 × 10 cm (3¾ × 3¾ in)
Thread: DMC embroidery floss. Use
2 strands in the needle

◪ 310 black

〜 310 (backstitch)

⊡ 3781 brown

— 3023 beige

CUSHION WITH INSECTS

Material: linen, 8 threads per cm (20 threads per in)
Cutting size: 45 × 50 cm (17¾ × 19½ in)
Finished size: 38 × 43 cm (15 × 17 in)
Zipper: 30 cm (11¾ in)
Thread: DMC embroidery floss. Use 3 strands in the needle

- ◣ 905 green
- ■ 831 dark gold
- — 831 (backstitch)
- ⊙ 972 yellow
- ⊠ 797 dark blue
- ⅃ 799 light blue

WALLHANGING WITH WREATHED BUTTERFLIES

Material: linen, 10 threads per cm
(25 threads per in)
Cutting size: 25 × 28 cm (9¾ × 11 in)
Finished size: 19 × 22.5 cm
(7½ × 8¾ in)
Piece of cardboard: 19 × 22.5 cm
(7½ × 8¾ in)
Thread: DMC embroidery floss. Use
2 strands in the needle

Wreath including butterfly (Lysandra bellargus)

- 320 green
- 368 light green
- 471 light yellowish green
- 645 dark grey
- — 645 (backstitch)
- 340 lavender
- 809 light blue

Upper butterfly (Hypolimnas misippus)

- 3021 dark brown
- ~~ 3021 (backstitch)
- 780 light brown
- — 780 (backstitch)
- 721 orange
- 741 dark yellow
- 742 light yellow
- white

Lower butterfly (Appias nero)

- 3021 dark brown
- ~~ 3021 (backstitch)
- 780 light brown
- — 780 (backstitch)
- 921 dark orange
- 721 light orange
- 741 yellow

To finish, count 9 threads from the border and fold the fabric under all round to make a neat edge. Glue in place on the cardboard.

Butterfly from Alaska
(Papilio machaon)

Material: linen, 10 threads per cm
(25 threads per in)
Design size: 15 × 22 cm (5¾ × 8¾ in)
Thread: DMC embroidery floss. Use
2 strands in the needle

◣ 310 black

— 310 (backstitch)

◿ 934 darkest green

⊡ 936 dark green

◩ 987 medium green

⟑ 989 light green

⌐ 471 lightest green

‖ 732 dull green

⊠ 833 gold

⊂ 743 yellow

⊙ 930 dull blue

⊠ 720 rust

⊟ 327 dark lilac

⊞ 553 medium lilac

⊿ 554 light lilac

Butterfly from the Solomon Islands
(Ornithoptera priamus)

Material: linen, 10 threads per cm (25 threads per in)
Design size: 16.5×21 cm ($6\frac{1}{2} \times 8\frac{1}{4}$ in)
Thread: DMC embroidery floss. Use 2 strands in the needle

- ◣   310 black
- —   310 (backstitch)
- ◿   898 dark brown
- ⊞   434 medium brown
- ⊙   680 gold
- ⧄   783 yellow
- ⊙   905 dark green
- ⌃   907 light green
- ⫼   734 light dull yellowish green
- ⊟   3051 dark grey
- ⊠   3053 light grey
- ■   347 dark red
- ⧅   351 medium red
- ⌑   352 light red

PLACEMAT WITH BUTTERFLIES

Material: Aida, $5\frac{1}{2}$ stitches per cm ($13\frac{1}{2}$ stitches per in)
Cutting size: 45×35 cm ($17\frac{3}{4} \times 13\frac{3}{4}$ in)
Finished size: 40×30 cm ($15\frac{3}{4} \times 11\frac{3}{4}$ in)
Thread: DMC embroidery floss. Use 2 strands in the needle

PLATE LINER

Material: Aida, $5\frac{1}{2}$ stitches per cm ($13\frac{1}{2}$ stitches per in)
Cutting size: 20×20 cm (8×8 in)
Finished size: 16.5×16.5 cm ($6\frac{1}{2} \times 6\frac{1}{2}$ in)
Thread: DMC embroidery floss. Use 2 strands in the needle

■ 838 dark brown
— 838 (backstitch)
⊙ 839 medium brown
⋰ 842 beige
◣ 580 dull green
⊠ 906 bright green
Ⅼ 907 light bright green
▨ 900 red
∼ 900 (backstitch)
◹ 972 yellow

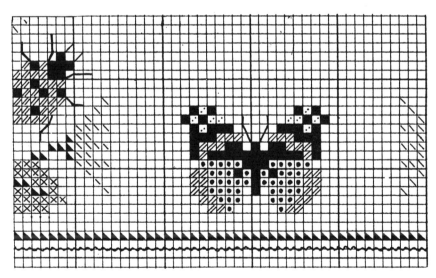

TABLE CENTREPIECE WITH BUTTERFLIES
(Anthocharis cardamines)

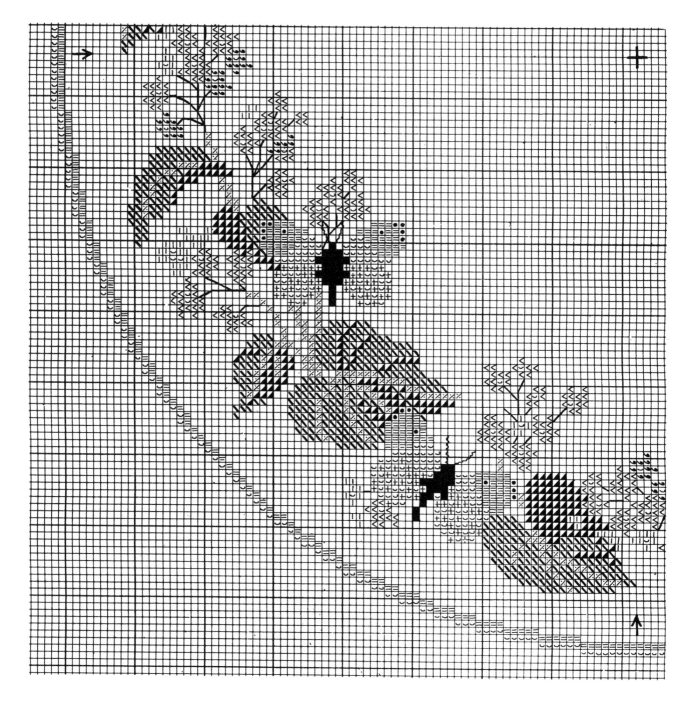

Material: Aida, 5½ stitches per cm (13½ stitches per in)
Cutting size: 38 × 38 cm (15 × 15 in)
Finished size: about 33 × 33 cm (13 × 13 in)
Lace: 120 cm (47 in)
Thread: DMC embroidery floss. Use 2 strands in the needle

◣ 988 dark green
◪ 3347 medium green
◨ 471 light green
— 471 (backstitch)
■ 3021 dark brown
⁓ 3021 (backstitch)
◉ 433 brown

⊞ 644 beige
⫼ 740 orange
〔 744 light yellow
〔 798 dark blue
∧ 799 light blue
⊟ 340 light lavender

BOOKMARK WITH BUTTERFLY

Material: linen, 8 threads per cm
(20 threads per in)
Cutting size: 18×9 cm ($7 \times 3\frac{1}{2}$ in)
Finished size: 18×3.5 cm ($7 \times 1\frac{1}{2}$ in)
Thread: DMC embroidery floss. Use
3 strands in the needle

- ● 988 green
- — 988 (backstitch)
- ▨ 553 lilac (or 603 rose)
- ■ 840 brown
- ∼ 840 (backstitch)
- ☒ 972 dark yellow (or 798 dark
  blue)
- Ⅼ 725 light yellow (or 799 light
  blue)

Iron the finished embroidery. Fold
the long edges to the wrong side,
overlap slightly and stitch neatly in
place. Make a fringe of about 1.5 cm
($\frac{1}{2}$ in) at the top and bottom by
removing threads.

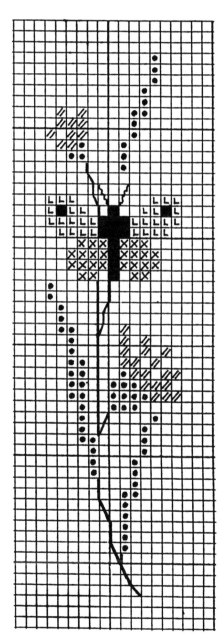

BUTTERFLY MOTIF FOR TOWEL

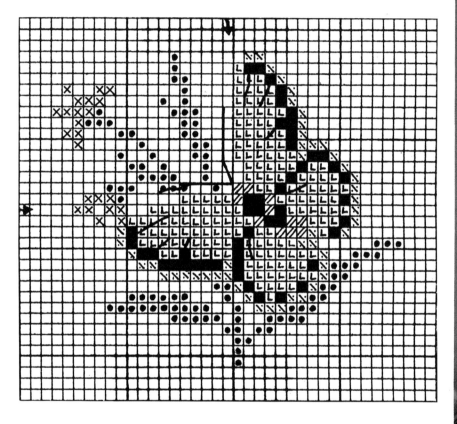

Material: piece of canvas about
12 × 12 cm (4¾ × 4¾ in) with 4 stitches
per cm (10 stitches per in)
Design size: 8.5 × 8 cm (3¼ × 3 in)
Thread: DMC embroidery floss. Use
6 strands in the needle

You can work the embroidery on
non–evenweave fabric by using waste
canvas. Follow the instructions on
page 10.

- ⊡ 906 green
- ■ 535 dark grey
- — 535 (backstitch)
- ▨ 312 dark blue
- Ⅼ 799 medium blue
- ◳ 775 light blue
- ⊠ 309 red

FRAMED BUTTERFLY I

(Gonepteryx rhamni)

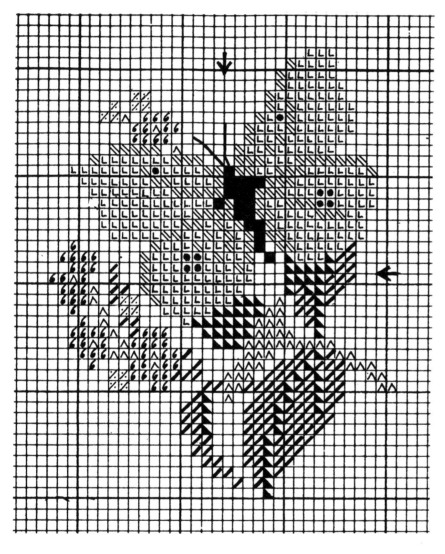

Material: linen, 10 threads per cm (25 threads per in)
Cutting size: 10×12 cm ($3\frac{3}{4} \times 4\frac{3}{4}$ in)
Frame (inside): 6×8 cm ($2\frac{1}{2} \times 3$ in)
Thread: DMC embroidery floss. Use 2 strands in the needle

◥ 3346 dark green

◿ 470 light green

△ 734 light dull green

■ 610 brown

● 970 orange

◩ 444 dark yellow

L 307 light yellow

₍ 553 dark lilac

◿ 554 light lilac

Iron the finished embroidery and fit into the frame.

FRAMED BUTTERFLY II

(Colias myrmidone)

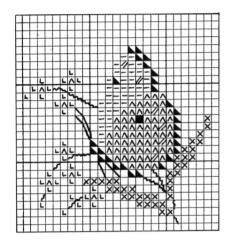

Material: linen, 10 threads per cm
(25 threads per in)
Cutting size: 10×10 cm ($3\frac{3}{4} \times 3\frac{3}{4}$ in)
Frame (inside): 6×6 cm ($2\frac{1}{2} \times 2\frac{1}{2}$ in)
Thread: DMC embroidery floss. Use
2 strands in the needle

■   3021 dark brown

◣   632 reddish brown

—   632 (backstitch)

⊼   725 dark yellow

⊟   726 light yellow

▨   832 gold

⁓   732 yellowish green (backstitch)

☒   3347 green

Ⓛ   3608 rose

Iron the finished embroidery and fit
into the frame.

FRAMED BUTTERFLY III
(Plebejus argus)

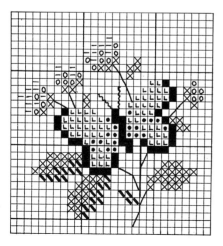

Material: linen, 10 threads per cm (25 threads per in)
Cutting size: 10×10 cm ($3\frac{3}{4} \times 3\frac{3}{4}$ in)
Frame (inside): 6×6 cm ($2\frac{1}{2} \times 2\frac{1}{2}$ in)
Thread: DMC embroidery floss. Use 2 strands in the needle

- ■ 610 brown
- ⌣ 610 (backstitch)
- ◩ 580 dark green
- ⊠ 470 light green
- — 470 (backstitch)
- ⊙ 972 dark yellow
- ⊟ 725 light yellow
- ◉ 414 grey
- ⊡ 799 blue

Iron the finished embroidery and fit into the frame.

6

Fish

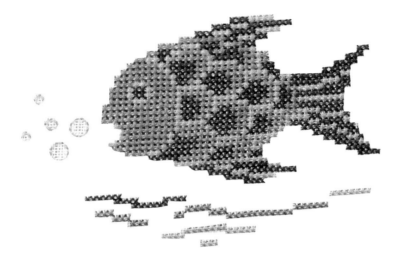

CUSHION WITH FISH

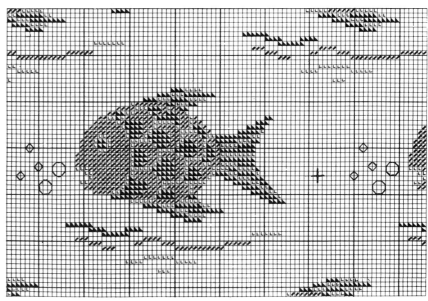

Material: linen, 10 threads per cm
(25 threads per in)
Cutting size: 48 × 40 cm
(19 × 15¾ in)
Finished size: 43 × 35 cm
(17 × 13¾ in)
Zipper: 30 cm (11¾ in)
Cord: about 200 cm (79 in)
Thread: DMC embroidery floss. Use
2 strands in the needle

◥ 797 dark blue

◪ 807 dark turquoise

ⓛ 598 light turquoise

— 598 (backstitch)

FRAMED AQUARIUM FISH
(Paracanthus hepatus and *Amphiprion ephippium)*

Material: linen, 10 threads per cm
(25 threads per in)
Cutting size: 30 × 30 cm
(11¾ × 11¾ in)
Frame (inside): 21.5 × 21.5 cm
(8½ × 8½ in)
Thread: DMC embroidery floss. Use
2 strands in the needle

◪ 580 dark green
☒ 732 light green
ㄴ 833 light gold
◣ 310 black
⊞ white
◉ 517 dark blue
Ⅲ 518 light blue

◺ 598 light turquoise
⊟ 900 dark orange
◿ 720 medium orange
◎ 740 light orange
◹ 725 yellow

Iron the finished embroidery and fit
it into the frame.

Sea-horse

Material: linen, 10 threads per cm
(25 threads per in)
Design size: 8 × 15 cm (3 × 5¾ in)
Thread: DMC embroidery floss. Use
2 strands in the needle

- ■ 420 brown
- ⧄ 680 light brown
- ⦀ 834 straw-yellow
- ⌊ 3047 light straw-yellow
- · 581 yellowish green
- ⊠ 470 green
- — 471 light green

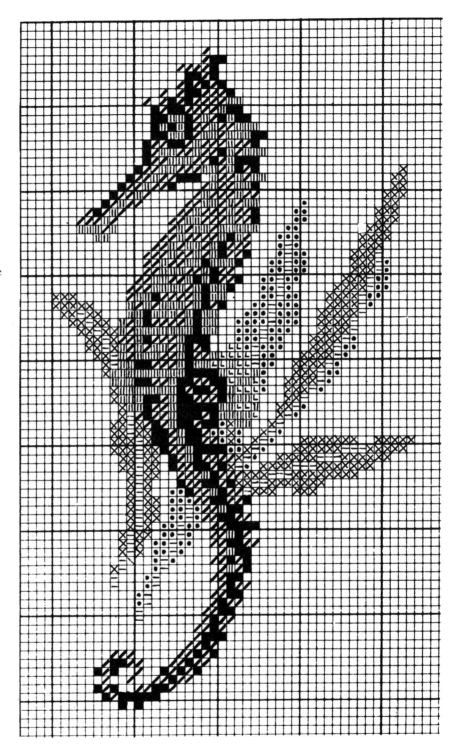